Stoner Calligraphy Workbook For Chill Creators

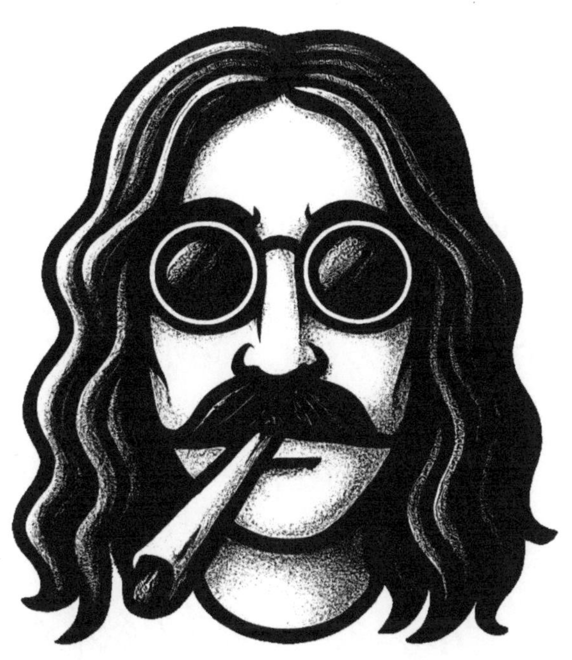

Disclaimer: This workbook is intended for artistic and recreational purposes only.

It does not promote or encourage the use of any controlled substances.

The content is not intended to provide medical advice or to serve as a therapeutic tool.

For health-related concerns or decisions, please consult a licensed medical professional.

How To Use This Workbook
(A.K.A. Let It Flow, Bro)

Hey, creative soul

This workbook ain't school — it's a chill session with the alphabet.
It's not about being perfect. It's about being you.

Step 1: Grab Your Tools

Pick up your favorite pen, marker, or pencil.
Something that feels right in your hand. (Bonus points if you've got a blunt in the other.)

Step 2: Trace it Slow

Don't rush. Calligraphy is like smoking a good joint — the slower, the better.
Follow the lines. Feel the rhythm.
Like you're sketching smoke in the air.

- Step 3: Mistakes? Dude, they're part of the vibe

Wobbly line? Nice. That's your style talking.

Calligraphy isn't rules — it's rhythm.

Every slip is a little signature of your groove.

- Step 4: Grow Your Flow

Start with letters. Then words. Then phrases.

Eventually? Full-on freestyle.

Create your own mantras. Posters. Doodles. Smoke-scented poetry.

- Step 5: Stay Chill

Throw on some chill beats. Light a candle. Sink into the moment.

This isn't about getting it done.

It's about feeling it.

Creative Vibes 101

Keep it easy, keep it breezy — stoner calligraphy isn't about strict rules or ancient techniques. It's all about chillin', flowing, and adding your own magic to every letter you draw. Here's the vibe: relaxed posture, a comfy grip, and the right paper can make your creativity fly. Mastering the basics will help you let your style float free and make your pen groove across the page.

Move with the Flow

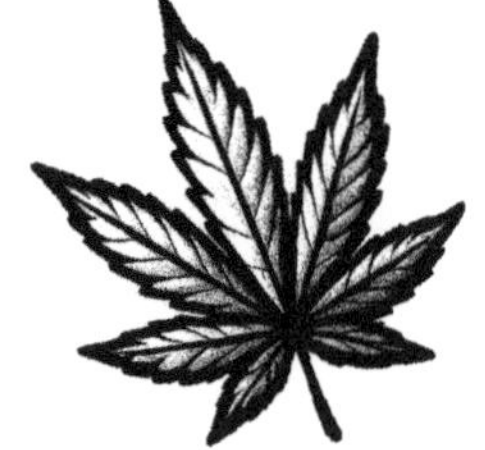

Think posture doesn't matter? Nah, think again, my friend.

In calligraphy (and life), being relaxed is everything.

Sit comfy — maybe on the floor, maybe at your favorite chill spot — and let your arm move easy and loose.

It's like a slow dance between you and the page: smooth, intentional, and totally free-flowing.

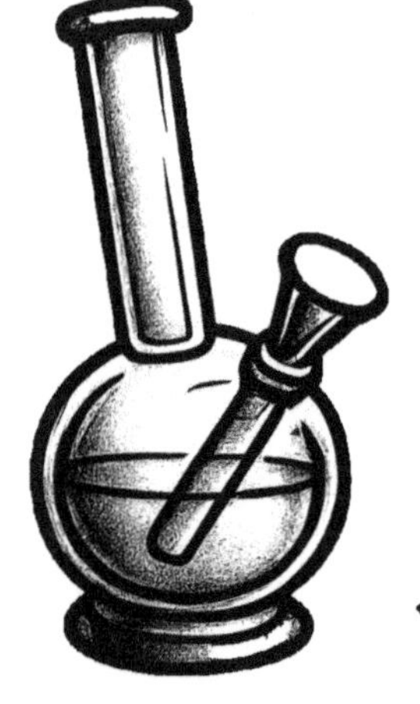

Your Magic Wand

Your pen is your portal to another dimension, dude.

Whether it's a brush pen, fineliner, or marker — pick what feels right.

Hold it easy, tilt it gently, and don't even think about perfection.

Wobbly lines? They're part of the journey.

Stoner calligraphy is all about vibing, learning, and letting your own unique flow take over naturally.

Chill Tools for Creative Souls

Feeling adventurous? There's a whole galaxy of tools out there — but no stress, you don't need 'em all.

Here's your starter pack:

★ Pencils

— humble, simple, perfect for sketching out your wild ideas.

★ Pens

— fineliners are a solid start. Trust the pen you vibe with the most.

★ Brush Pens

— the upgraded magic wands. Start small and get your groove going.

★ Watercolors

— wanna level up? Splash some color and watch your letters come alive.

Remember: It's all about playing, experimenting, and letting your creativity fly high.

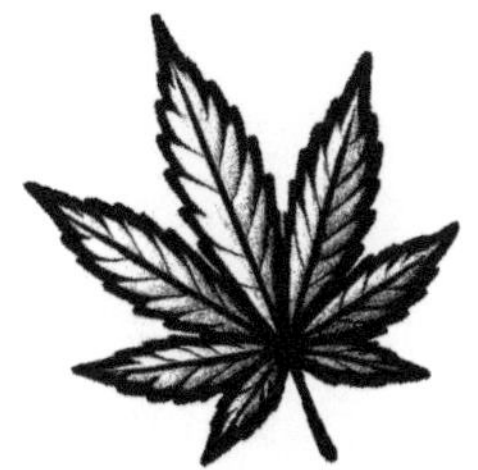

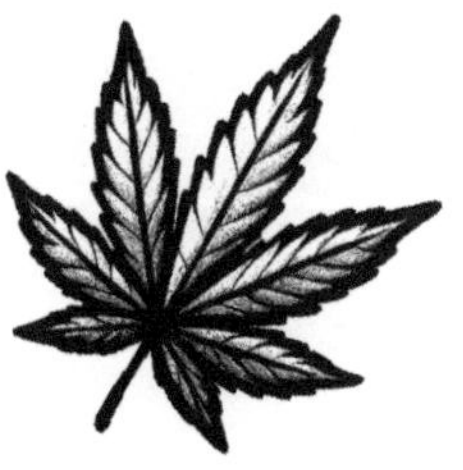

More Chill Tools for Your Flow

★ CHALK

CHALK MARKERS ARE TOTAL GAME-CHANGERS, DUDE. WITH A LITTLE FLOW AND SOME PRACTICE, YOU'LL BE LAYING DOWN THOSE DREAMY CHALKBOARD DESIGNS IN NO TIME. WHETHER IT'S CAFE MENUS OR SIDEWALK MASTERPIECES — CHALK CALLIGRAPHY HAS THAT RELAXED, ARTSY VIBE YOU'LL LOVE.

★ PAPER

THIS WORKBOOK GIVES YOU LOTS OF SPACE TO JAM, BUT EXPERIMENTING WITH DIFFERENT PAPERS CAN REALLY TUNE YOUR VIBE. HEAVIER STUFF LIKE CARDSTOCK MAKES YOUR STROKES SMOOTHER AND YOUR COLORS POP HARDER. STAY AWAY FROM SUPER THIN PRINTER PAPER — IT'S A REAL BUZZKILL FOR YOUR FLOW.

★ FUDENOSUKE PEN

THIS LITTLE MARKER IS LIKE THE SWISS ARMY KNIFE OF MONOLINE VIBES: CLEAN, SIMPLE, AND TOTALLY RELIABLE. IF YOU'RE STARTING OUT OR JUST WANT TO ZEN OUT WITH CRISP LINES, THIS PEN'S YOUR BEST BUD.

★ BRUSHES

BRUSH PENS = PURE MAGIC. PERFECT FOR BOLD STROKES, DREAMY FLOURISHES, OR TRIPPY LITTLE ACCENTS. PLAY WITH THEM, MIX IT UP, AND LET YOUR LETTERS GROOVE HOWEVER THEY WANT.

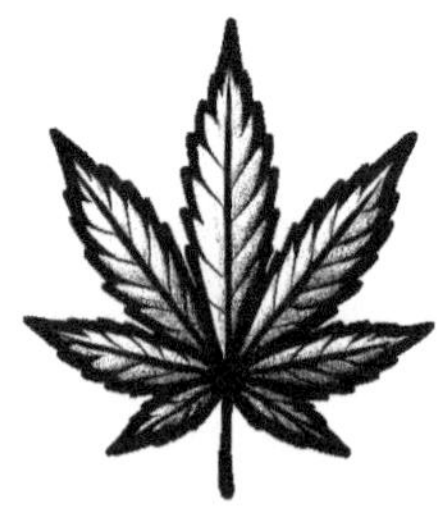

Talk the Chill Talk: Groovy Terms

Before you start creating those beautiful, relaxed letters, it's good to know some basic lingo.

Think of it as learning the language of flow — it'll make your creative trip way smoother.

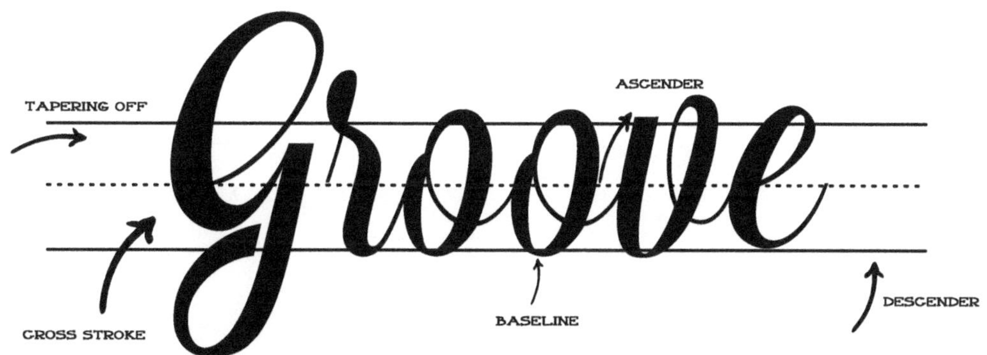

★ **DESCENDING STROKE**

A downward stroke that adds juicy weight and boldness to your letters.

★ **ASCENDING STROKE**

An upward stroke that keeps things light, graceful, and full of good vibes.

★ **ASCENDER**

The high-flying part of a letter, like the top of a "T" or "H".

★ **DESCENDER**

The part that dips low, like the tail of a "G" or "Y" — going with the flow.

★ **FLOW**

Cool extra lines, swirls, or arrows that give your letters personality and soul.

★ **CROSSBAR**

The horizontal stroke in letters like "T", "F", or "H" — balancing your vibes.

★ **LETTERFORM**

The full shape and soul of a letter — your unique style in every curve.

Groovy Writing Tips

★ ONE

Take it slow, friend. Every letter's a little piece of magic.
No rushin' — just flowin'. Let your pen cruise like it's vibin' with the page.

★ TWO

Start with a pencil — your low-pressure buddy. Sketch, chill, refine.
Mistakes? Totally part of the journey, man.

★ THREE

Lift your pen after every stroke. This ain't cursive class — it's chill calligraphy.
One line at a time, full control, total calm.

★ FOUR

Golden rule? Downstrokes are thicker — like heavy beats in your favorite track.
It's the contrast that makes it pop.

★ FIVE

Upstrokes? Think light as air. Let your hand float.
You're gliding, not grinding.

★ SIX

Practice is the trip. Letters, words, funky compositions — it's all a vibe.
Let your flow evolve and your style bloom.

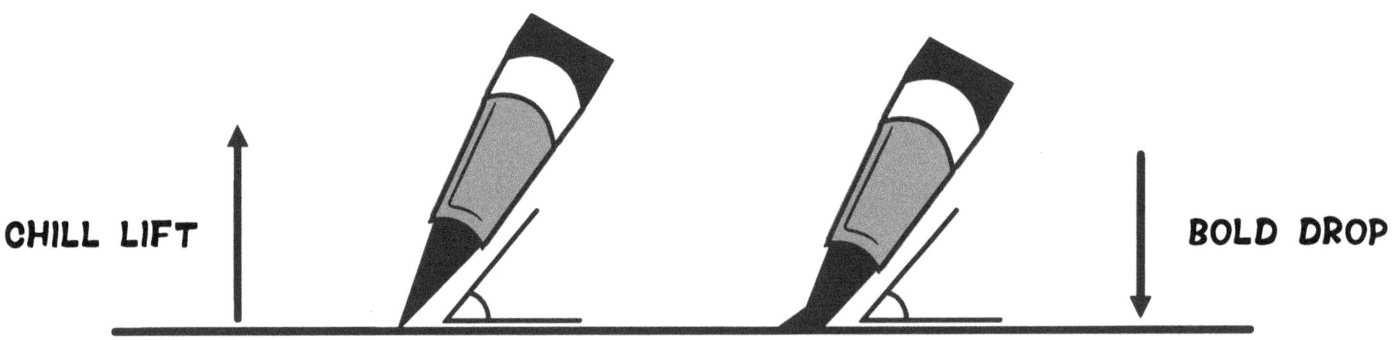

FEEL THE RHYTHM IN YOUR FINGERS!!!

Stroke Your Vibe

ALSO KNOWN AS FAUX CALLIGRAPHY, THESE STROKES ARE A GREAT PLACE TO START VIBIN'.

I'M ALL ABOUT MONOLINE — NO PRESSURE, JUST FLOW.

IT'S QUICKER, EASIER, AND LETS YOUR CREATIVE MIND BREATHE.

YOU'LL MIMIC THE BRUSH LETTERING MOVES, BUT KEEP THE PRESSURE CHILL AND STEADY.

NO THICK PUSH-DOWNS HERE. JUST GRAB A PENCIL OR FINELINER AND GROOVE AWAY.

THE SMALLER THE TIP, THE SMOOTHER THE TRIP.

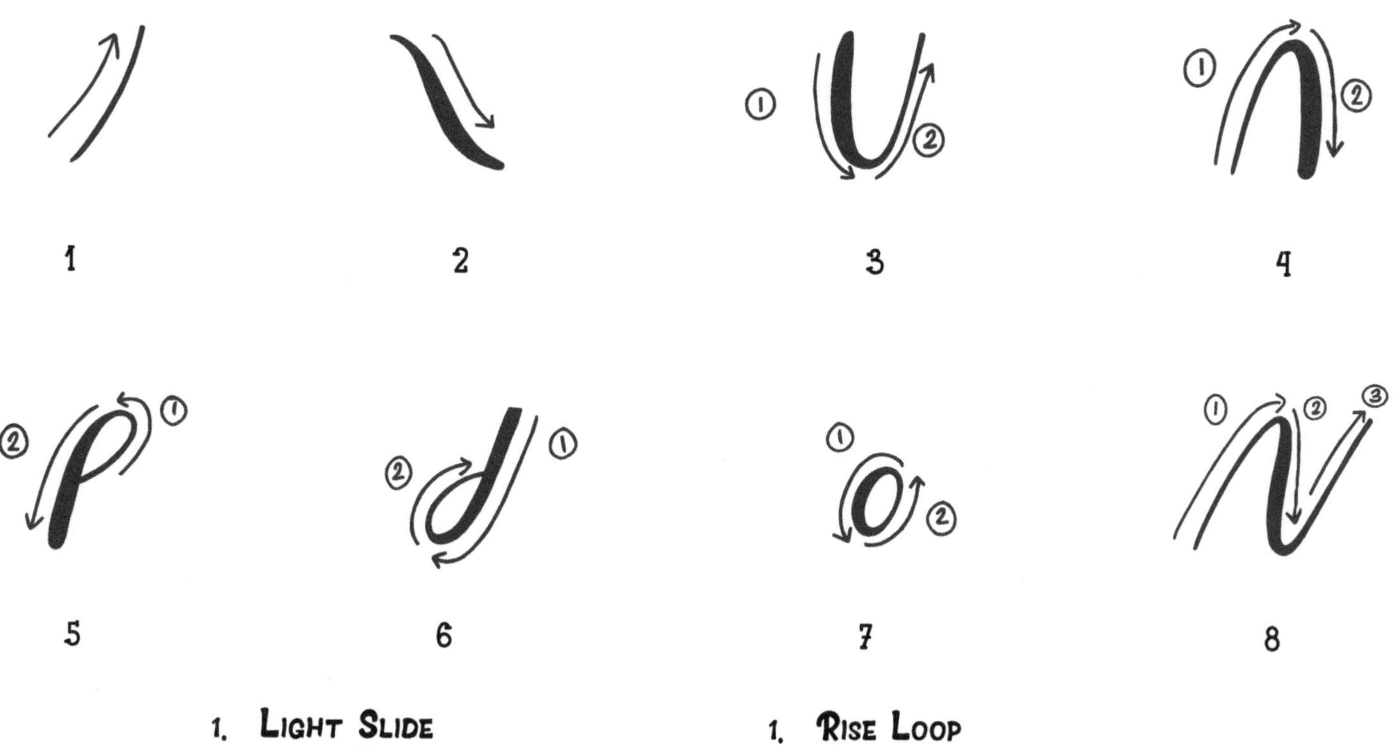

1. LIGHT SLIDE
2. LOW RIPPLE
3. BACKSPIN
4. FLIP FLOW

1. RISE LOOP
2. DROP CURVE
3. CHILL OVAL
4. FUNKY CURVE

Light Slide

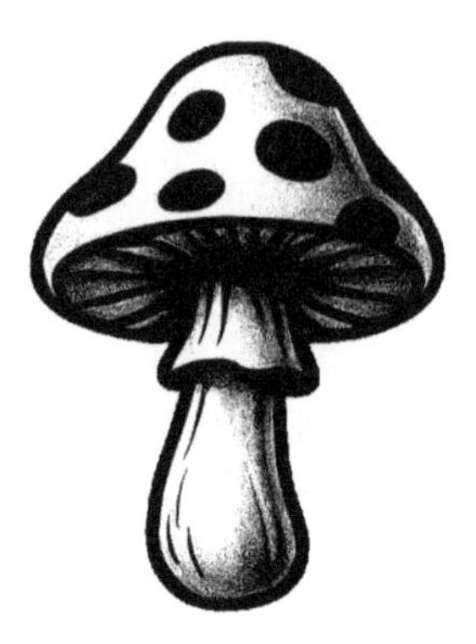

- START LOW AND FLOAT YOUR PEN UP LIKE A RISING VIBE.

- KEEP IT THIN AND SMOOTH — NO PRESSURE (LITERALLY).

- GENTLE TOUCH = GRACEFUL GROOVE.

Bold Drop

- THIS TIME, START FROM THE TOP AND LET GRAVITY DO ITS THING.

- ADD SOME CHILL WEIGHT AS YOU FLOW DOWN — BOLD, STEADY, MELLOW.

- EASE UP AT THE END LIKE A LEAF LANDING SOFT.

Sky Loop

- LET YOUR PEN RISE SMOOTH AND LIGHT — LIKE SMOKE CURLING UPWARD.

- THIS STROKE IS ALL ABOUT GENTLE MOTION AND STAYING RELAXED.

- KEEP IT STEADY, DON'T FORCE IT — THE MAGIC IS IN THE FLOW.

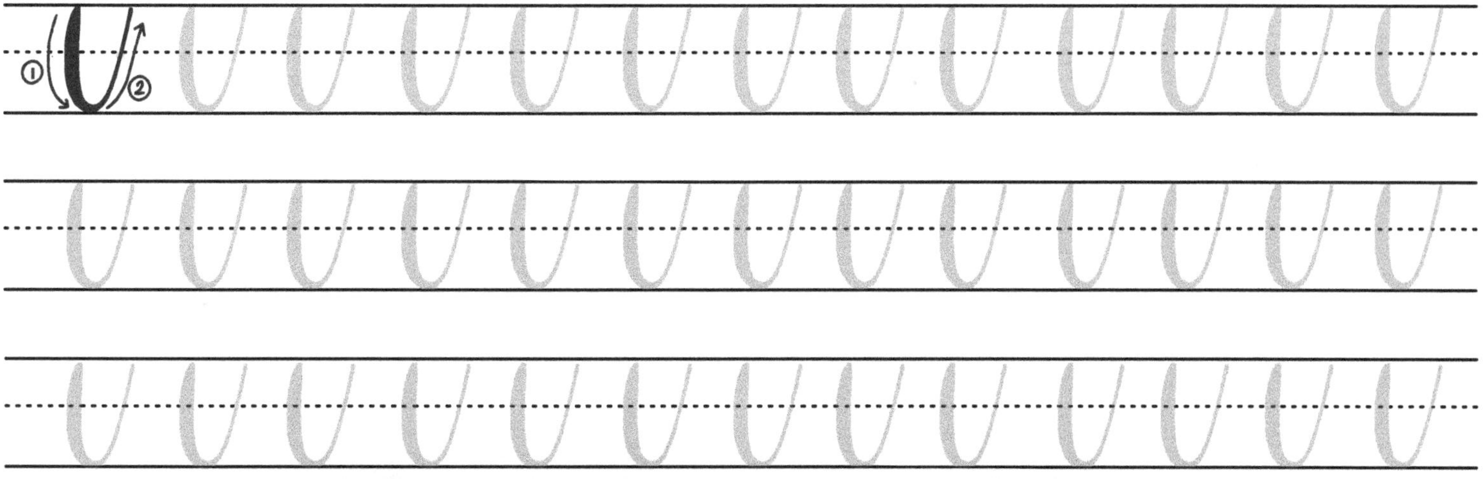

The Chill Flip

- BEGIN WITH A SOFT RISE — STEADY AND LIGHT.

- GENTLY MELT INTO A THICKER, SMOOTH DESCENT.

- THE KEY? FLOW LIKE SMOKE. LET THE SHIFT BE SEAMLESS AND SATISFYING.

Rise Loop

- LET YOUR PEN FLOAT UPWARD IN A MELLOW LOOP — LIKE SMOKE RISING IN A SPIRAL. KEEP YOUR LINES LIGHT AND SMOOTH. THIS STROKE BUILDS GRACE AND BALANCE INTO YOUR LETTERS. LET IT LIFT YOU.

Drop Curve

NOW TAKE IT LOW. LET YOUR PEN FLOW DOWNWARD IN A SOFT ARC. ADD GENTLE PRESSURE AS YOU MOVE, LIKE THE RHYTHM SLOWING DOWN. IT'S ALL ABOUT CONTROL AND CHILL DESCENT

Chill Oval

IMAGINE DRAWING LAZY O'S IN THE AIR — EVEN,SMOOTH, NO RUSH. THESE SHAPES BUILD THE SOUL OF YOUR LETTERS. BREATHE IN,TRACE THE CURVE, AND LET IT GO.

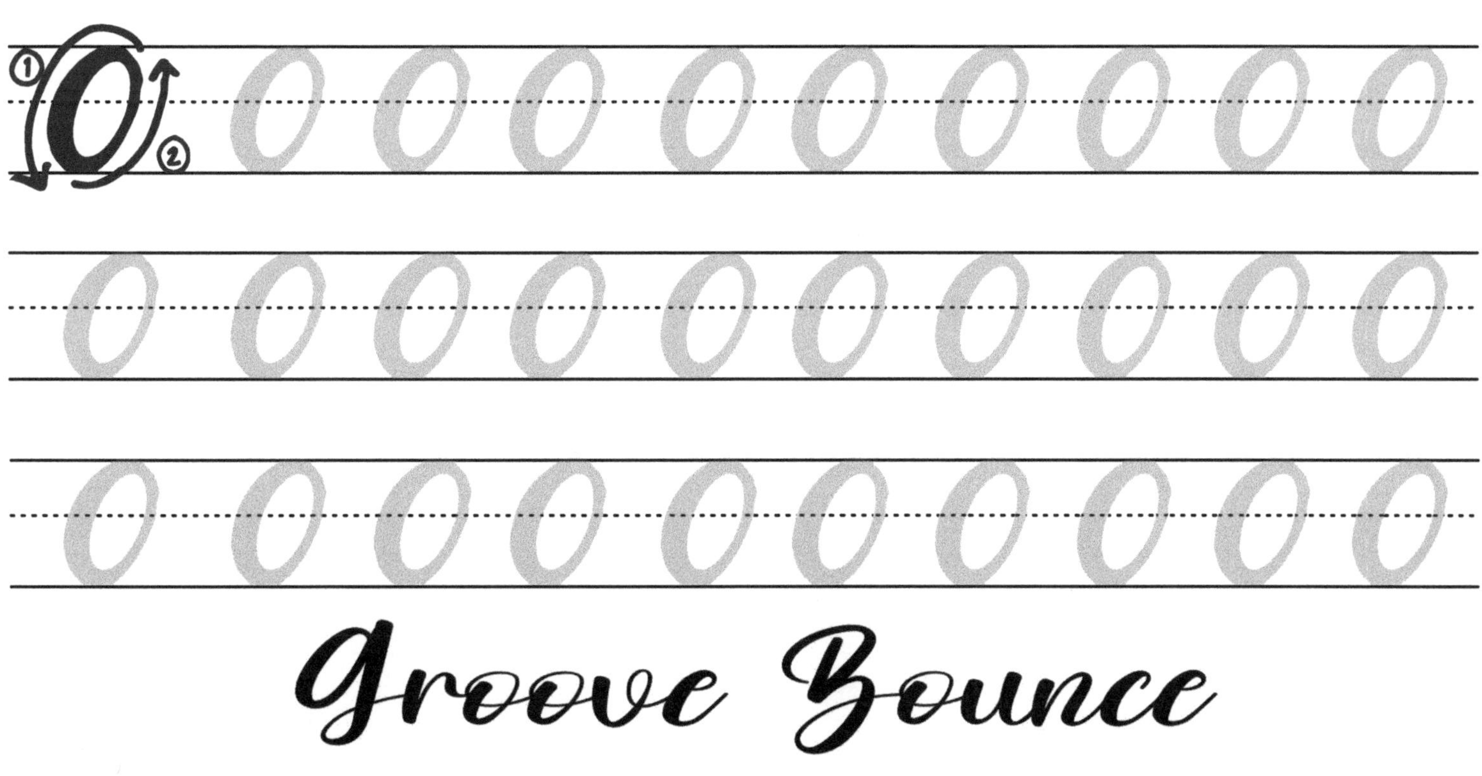

Groove Bounce

TIGHT TURNS, FLOWING MOTION — THIS IS YOUR BOUNCE. KEEP YOUR SPACING GROOVY AND CONSISTENT. IT'S LIKE A LETTER DANCE WITH A MELLOW BEAT. FLOW IN,CURVE OUT.

Chill Caps — Flow Your ABCs

UPPERCASE ALPHABET — MELLOW PRACTICE, ONE LETTER AT A TIME

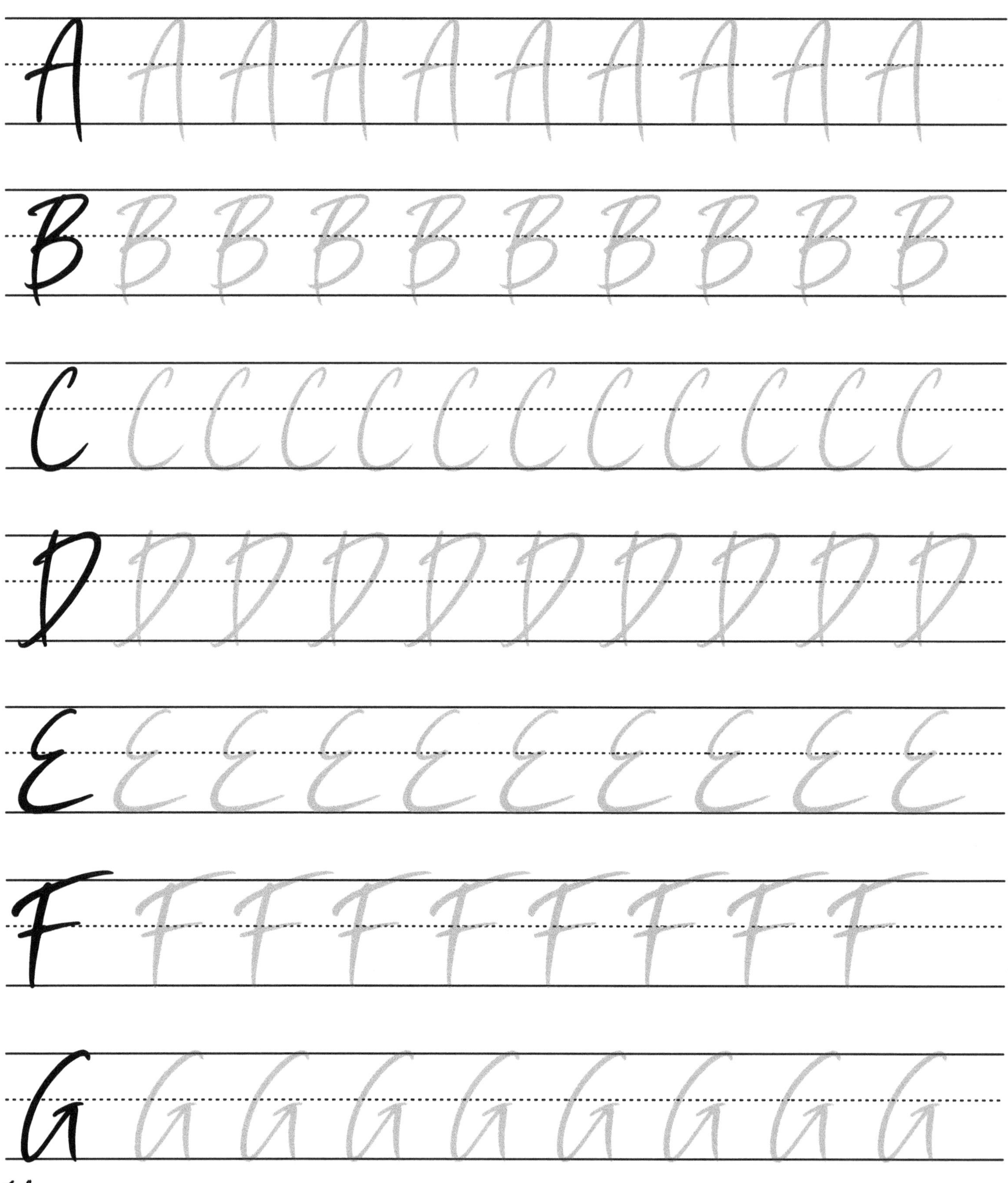

Your Groove Space

NO RULES HERE. PLAY, EXPLORE, AND LET YOUR HAND DO ITS THING.

REPEAT THE LETTERS. MIX THEM, ADD LOOPS. JUST FLOW

Chill Caps — Flow Your ABCs

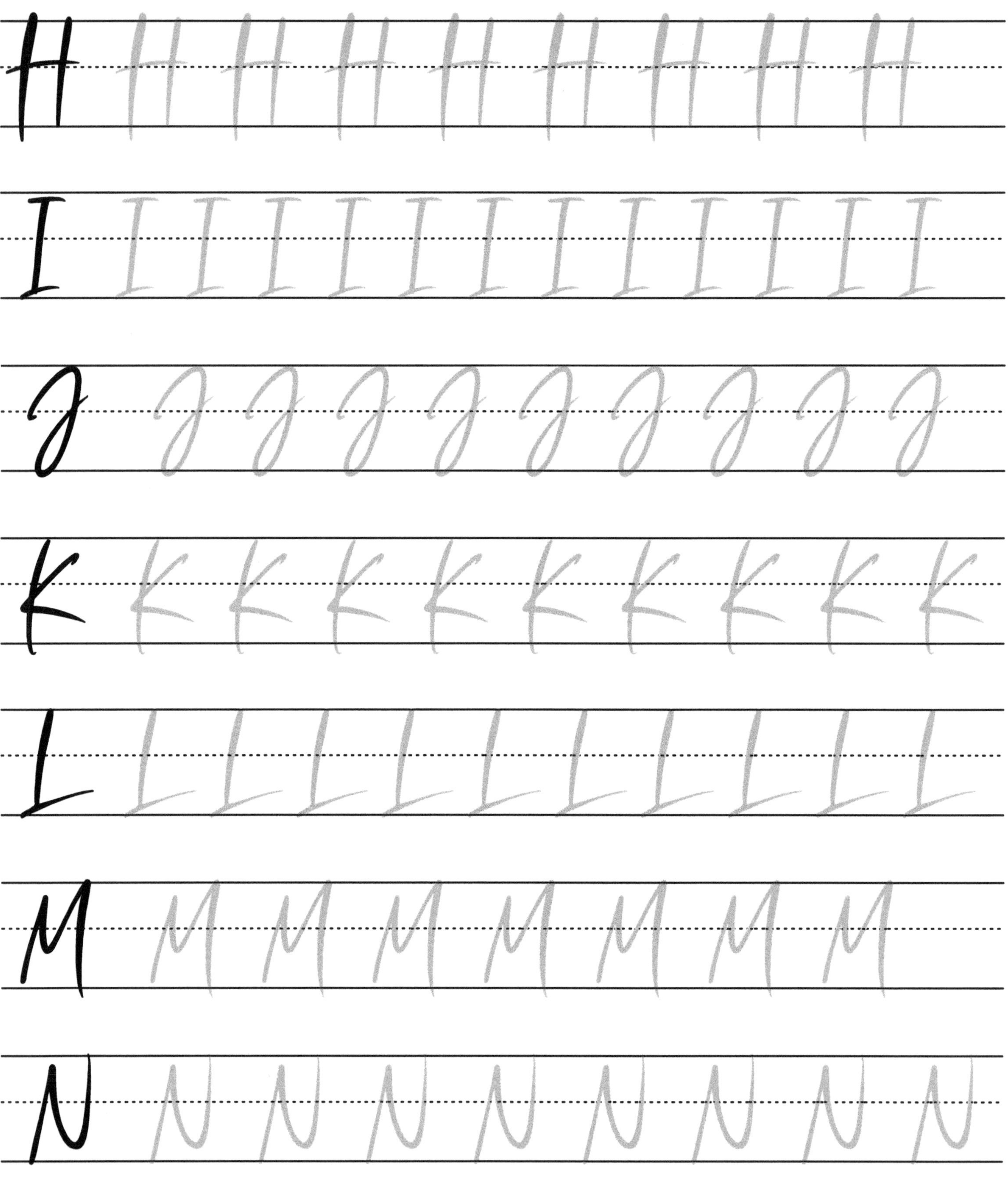

Your Groove Space

Chill Caps — Flow Your ABCs

O TO U – TRACE IT, VIBE IT, OWN IT.

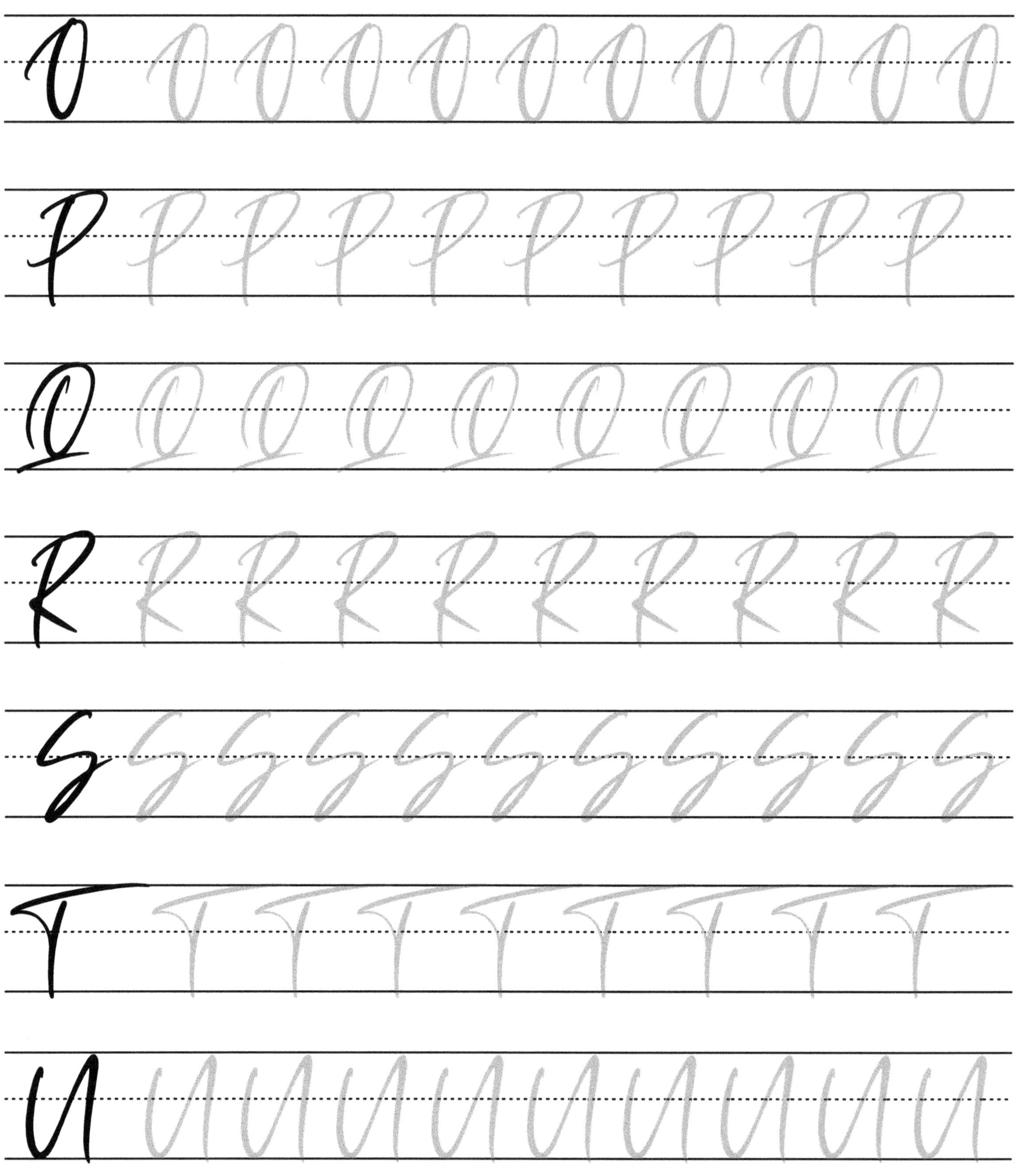

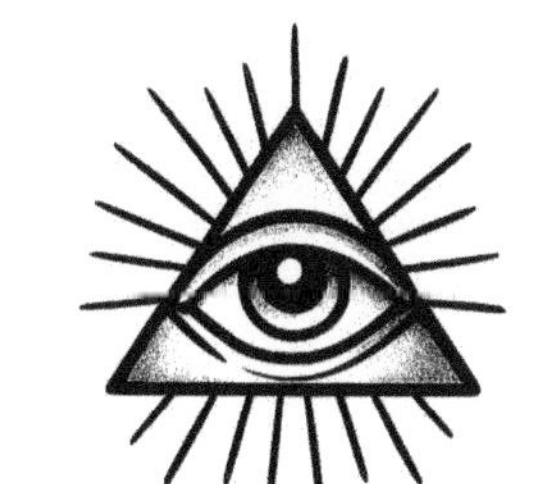

Chill Space

THIS IS YOUR PLACE TO JAM.
COMBINE LETTERS, MAKE WORDS — OR JUST LET YOUR HAND DRIFT.
NO RULES, ONLY RHYTHM.

Chill Caps — Flow Your ABCs

V TO Z – STILL VIBIN', STILL WRITIN'

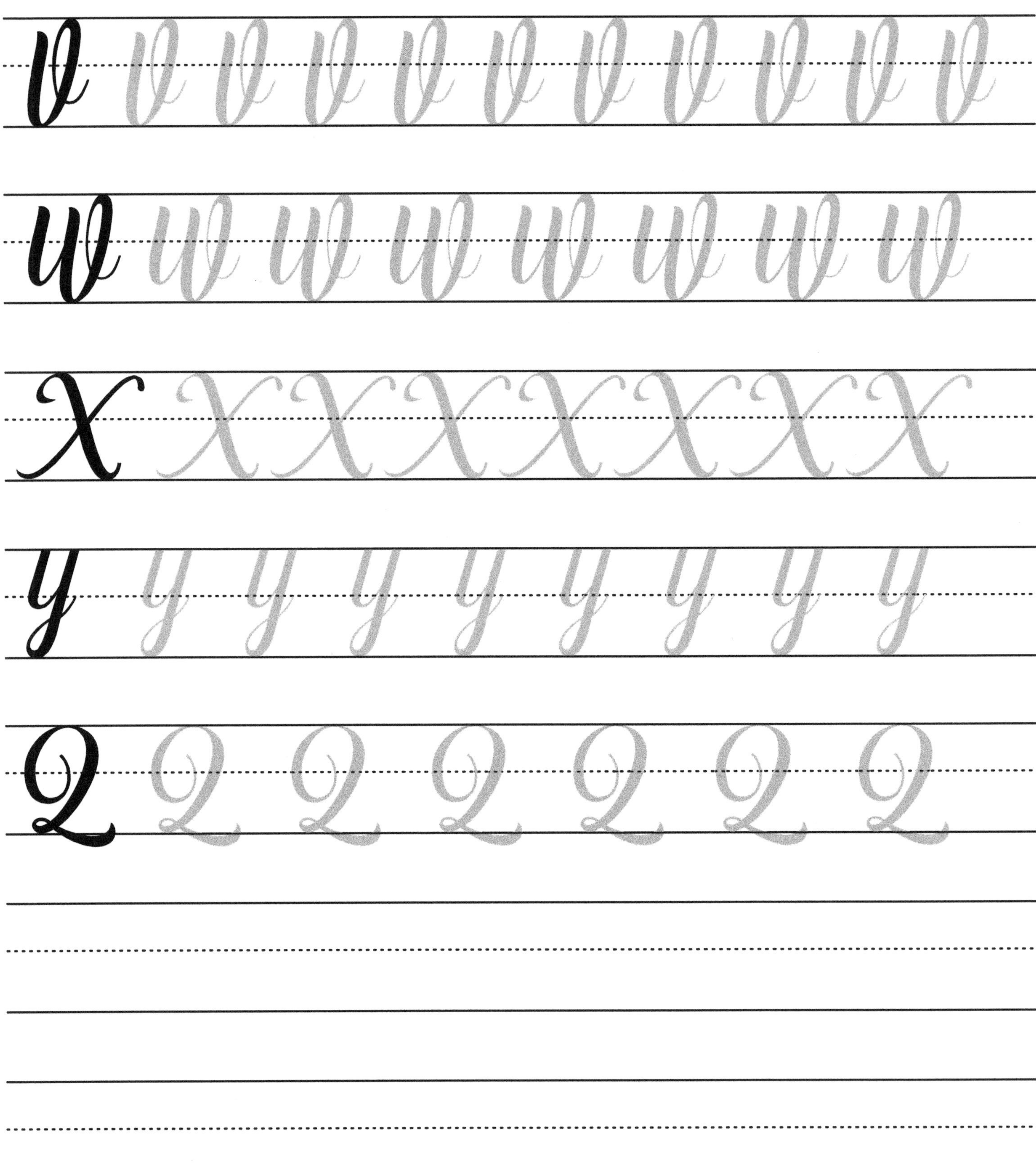

Freestyle Space

Smooth Letters — Let It Flow

A TO G — LITTLE LETTERS, BIG ENERGY

a *a a a a a a a a a a a a a a a a a a*

b *b b b b b b b b b b b b b b b b b b*

c *c c c c c c c c c c c c c c c c c c c*

d *d d d d d d d d d d d d d d d d d d*

e *e e e e e e e e e e e e e e e e e e*

f *f f f f f f f f f f f f f f f f f f f*

g *g g g g g g g g g g g g g g g g g g*

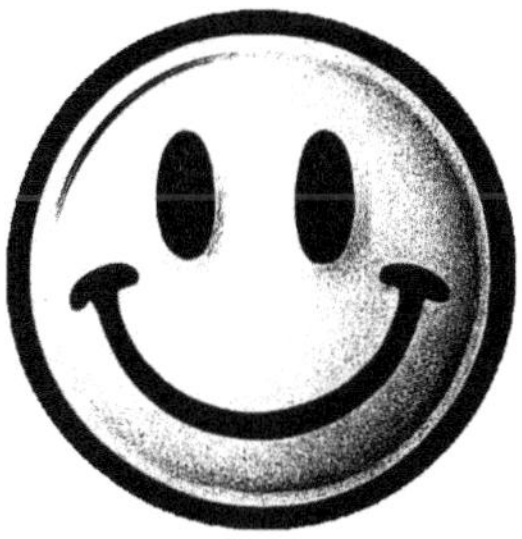

Mini Chill Space

REPEAT THE STROKES, SLOW YOUR BREATH.

ADD A SWIRL, FLIP A SHAPE, EXPLORE YOUR FLOW.

THAT'S WHAT IT'S ALL ABOUT.

Smooth Letters — Let It Flow

H TO N — CHILL LINES AND MELLOW CURVES

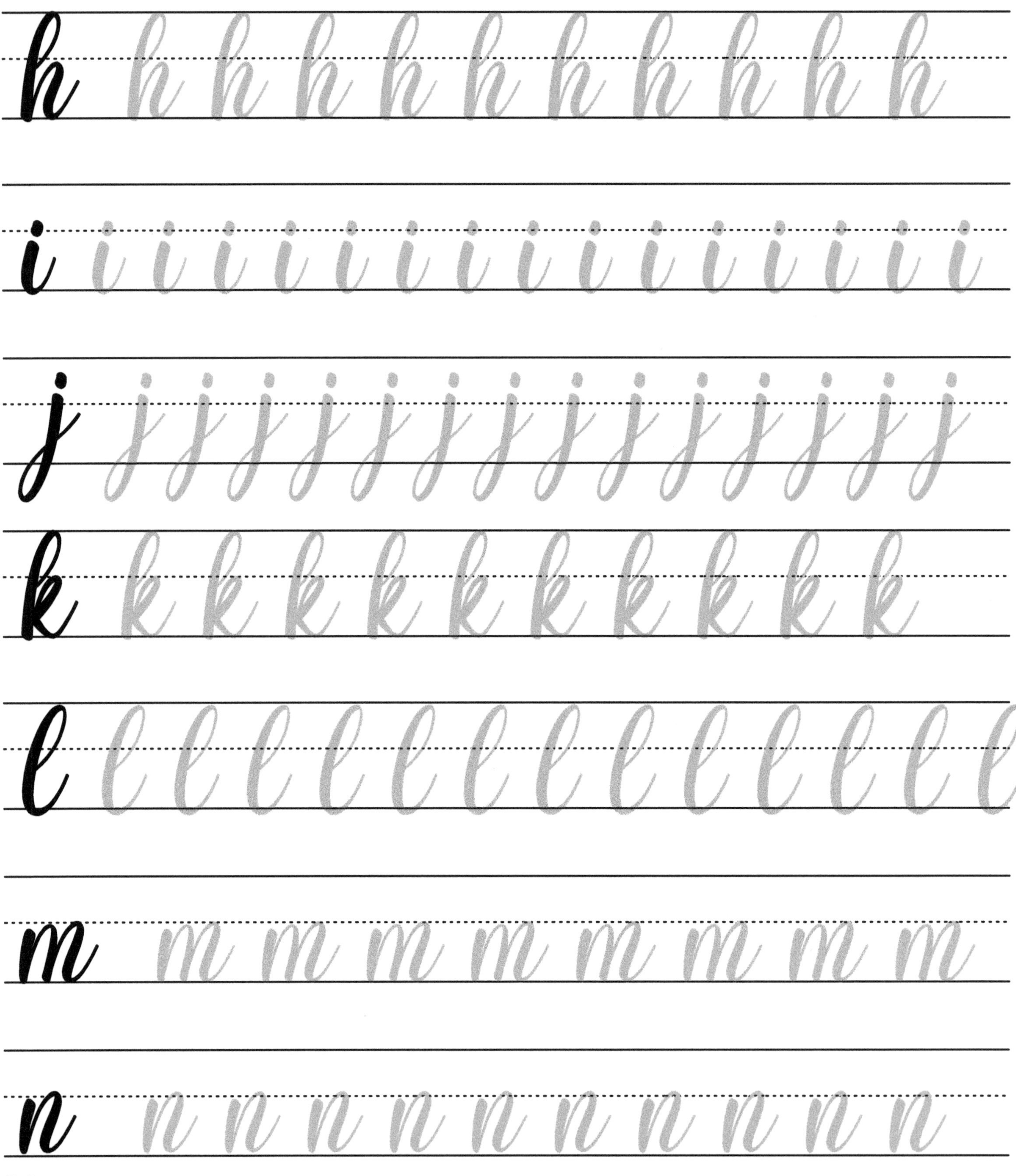

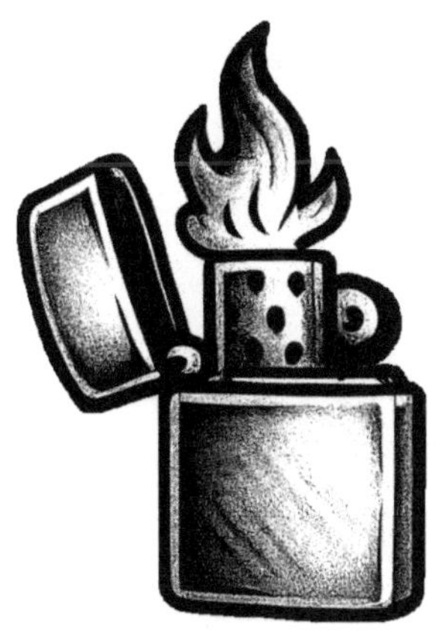

Flow Zone

YOU'RE HALFWAY THROUGH THE LOWER FLOW.
TIME TO CONNECT THE DOTS, SHAPE BY SHAPE.
TRUST YOUR VIBE.

Smooth Letters — Let It Flow

O TO U – LOOPY, LAZY, LOVELY LINES

Vibe Pad

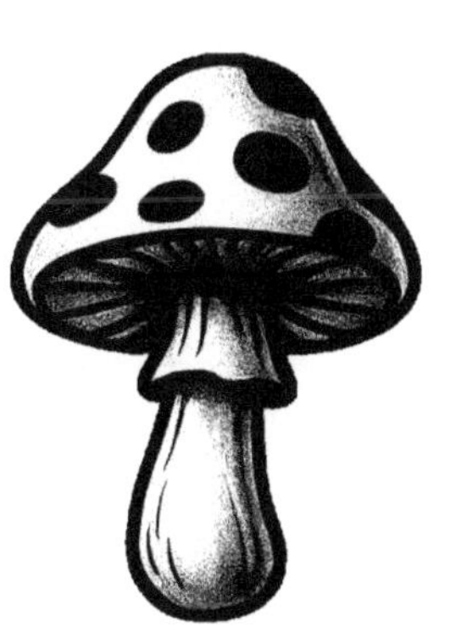

WANNA WRITE "PUFF", "PEACE", OR "SUN"?

GO AHEAD — THESE LETTERS GOT YOU.

LET THE WORDS ROLL OUT NATURALLY.

Total Flow Zone

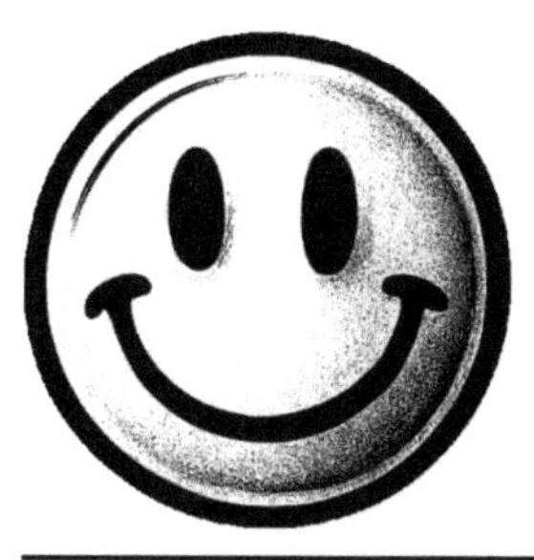

TRY WRITING YOUR NAME.

TRY THE WORD "ZEN".

TRY ANYTHING — JUST DON'T TRY TOO HARD.

Numbers Flow Too

0 0 0 0 0 0 0 0 0 0 0 0 0 0 0

1 1 1 1 1 1 1 1 1 1 1 1 1 1 1

2 2 2 2 2 2 2 2 2 2 2 2 2 2 2

3 3 3 3 3 3 3 3 3 3 3 3 3 3 3

4 4 4 4 4 4 4 4 4 4 4 4 4 4 4

5 5 5 5 5 5 5 5 5 5 5 5 5 5 5

6 6 6 6 6 6 6 6 6 6 6 6 6 6 6

TRY WRITING TIMES, BIRTHDAYS, CODES, OR NOTHING AT ALL.
DOODLE NUMBERS, CONNECT THEM, OR JUST BREATHE AND TRACE.

Numbers Flow Too

7 7 7 7 7 7 7 7 7 7 7 7 7

8 8 8 8 8 8 8 8 8 8 8 8 8 8

9 9 9 9 9 9 9 9 9 9 9 9 9

Free Countin' Zone

MIX NUMBERS WITH LETTERS.

TRACE YOUR FAVORITE TIME, WRITE 4:20 A FEW TIMES

OR JUST SCRIBBLE TIL YOUR MIND SAYS: "NICE"

Vibe

EVERY LETTER HAS ITS OWN RHYTHM.

LET YOUR PEN GLIDE LIKE SOUND THROUGH SMOKE.
TRACE IT SLOW, FEEL IT BUILD — THAT'S YOUR VIBE.

Vibe

Chill

Mellow

Glow

Breathe

Flow

Trace & Blaze

TRACE EACH WORD SLOWLY.

LET YOUR HAND RELAX AND FOLLOW THE RHYTHM.

REPEAT. GROOVE. ENJOY THE FLOW.

Lifted

LET EACH LETTER FLOAT LIKE SMOKE

NO RUSH, NO RULES, JUST RHYTHM IN THE AIR

High *High High High High*

Ease *Ease Ease Ease Ease*

Light *Light Light Light Light*

Sky *Sky Sky Sky Sky*

Cloud *Cloud Cloud Cloud*

Rise *Rise Rise Rise Rise Rise*

The Chill Zone

FOLLOW YOUR BREATH AS YOU TRACE

LET THE LETTERS RISE SLOWLY — LIGHT AS A CLOUD.

REPEAT UNTIL CALM FEELS NORMAL.

Waves

LET THE MOTION GUIDE YOU

UP, DOWN, AROUND — FEEL THE PULSE OF EVERY LINE.

Wave   Wave   Wave   Wave

Ripple   Ripple   Ripple   Ripple

Drift   Drift   Drift   Drift

Tide   Tide   Tide   Tide

Breeze   Breeze   Breeze   Breeze

Float   Float   Float   Float

Ink And Chill

MOVE LIKE WATER, WRITE LIKE WIND.

TRACE WITH EASE – LET THE INK DANCE ON ITS OWN.

Cosmic Drift

FLOAT THROUGH THE LETTERS

DON'T RUSH. LET YOUR PEN DRIFT LIKE STARDUST IN SLOW MOTION

Cosmic *Cosmic Cosmic Cosmic Cosmic*

Drift *Drift Drift Drift Drift*

Dream *Dream Dream Dream Dream*

Moon *Moon Moon Moon Moon*

Orbit *Orbit Orbit Orbit*

Space *Space Space Space Space*

THINK OF EACH STROKE AS A SHOOTING STAR.

BREATHE DEEP, TRACE SLOW — THE UNIVERSE IS IN YOUR HAND.

Higher Thoughts

LET YOUR MIND WANDER

TRACE THESE PHRASES LIKE YOU'RE WRITING IN SMOKE ON A LAZY AFTERNOON

Lost in thought

Let it be

Follow the breeze

Inhale the calm

Floating away

Peace of mind

Write the Vibe

Smoke

WEED

Everyday

Inner Flow

Breathe and release

Trust the process

Slow is smooth

Feel the moment

Mind like water

No rush needed

Mindful Lines

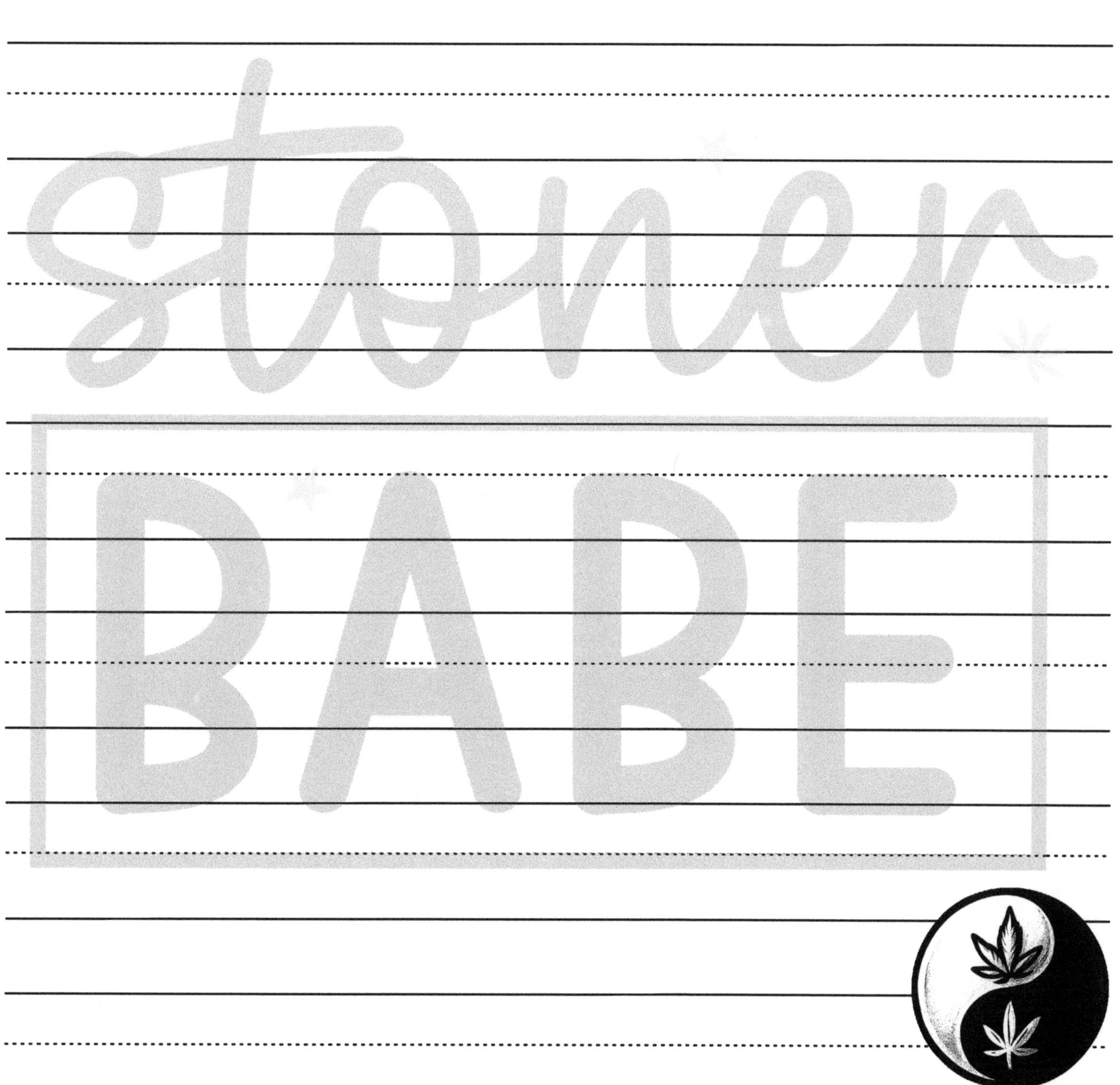

Slow Burn

LET THE LETTERS UNFOLD SLOWLY

TAKE YOUR TIME, LET THE WORDS SETTLE LIKE SMOKE IN THE AIR.

Stay a while

Take it slow

Enjoy the silence

No rush at all

Easy come, easy flow

Light and steady

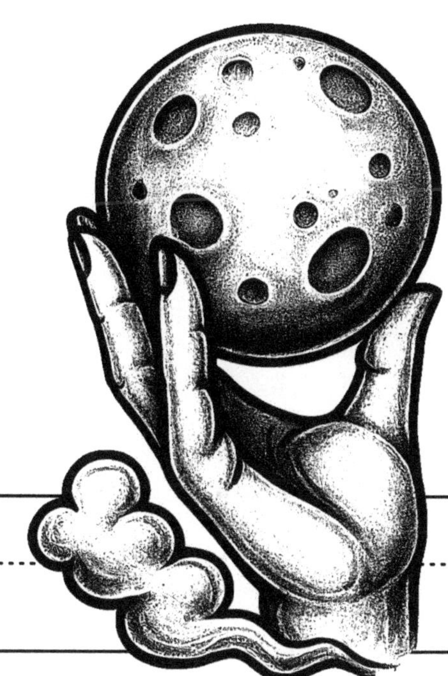

Flow Space

LET EACH PHRASE SINK IN AS YOU TRACE.

FEEL THE SHAPE, FEEL THE STILLNESS.

Good Vibes Only

High on life

Smile inside

Let joy grow

Feel the love

Everything is light

Calm and kind

TRACE WITH A SMILE. LET THE GOOD ENERGY SHOW IN EVERY CURVE.
YOU'RE NOT JUST WRITING – YOU'RE SHINING.

WORLD'S dopest DAD

Trace The Leaf

LET YOUR PEN FOLLOW THE FLOW OF NATURE.

TRACE IT SLOWLY – LIKE YOU'RE DRAWING SMOKE IN THE WIND.

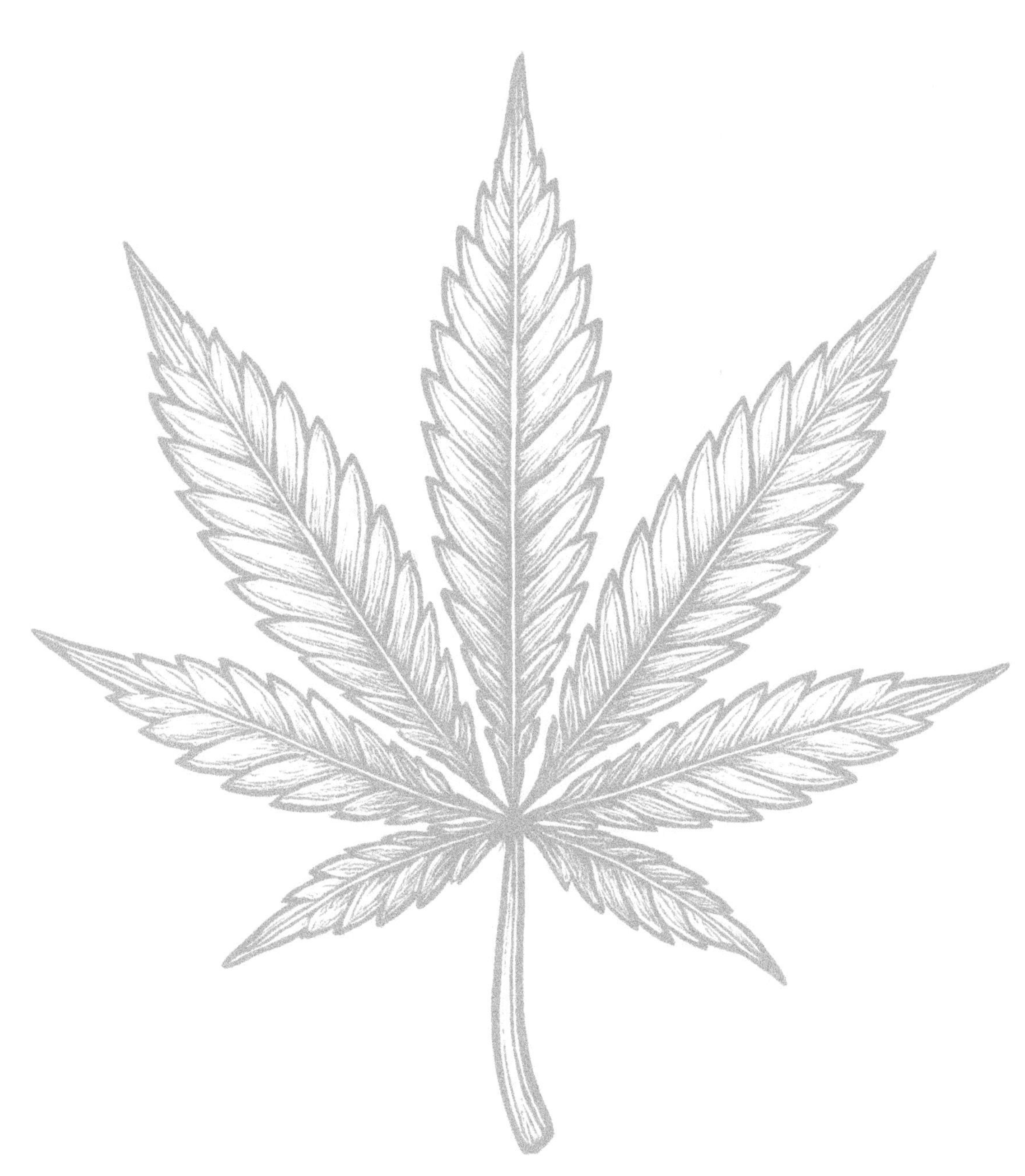

Drift With The Moon

FOLLOW EACH CURVE LIKE IT'S A DREAM LOOPING THROUGH THE NIGHT.

STAY CHILL, STAY LIGHT.

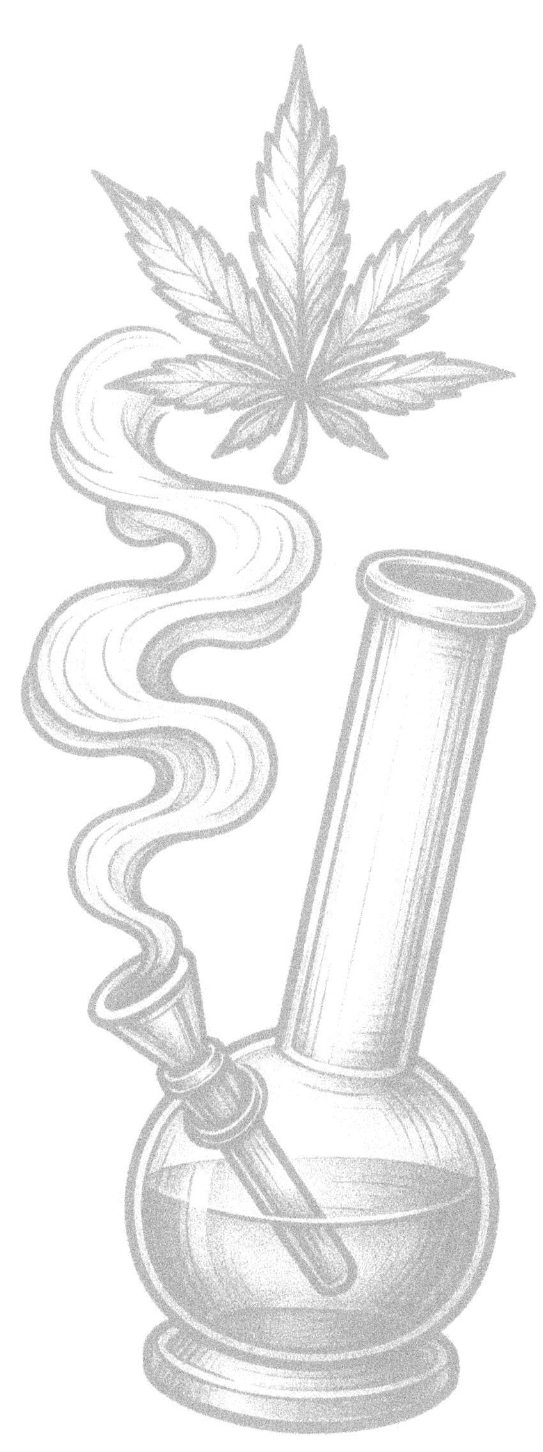

Smoke Spiral

TRACE THE SWIRLS – LET YOUR MIND FLOW WITH EVERY TWIST.

DON'T AIM FOR PERFECTION – JUST PRESENCE

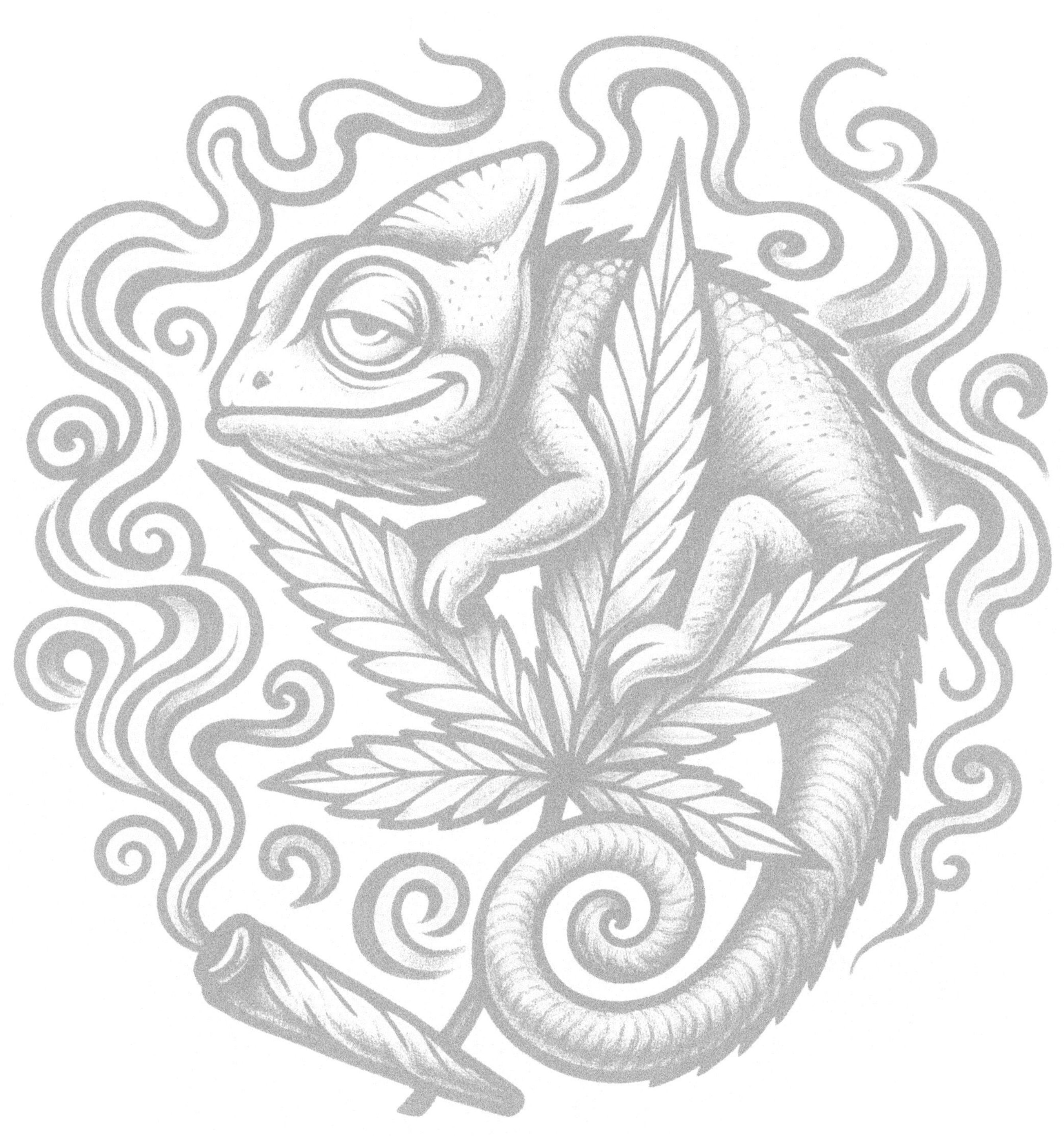

Blaze The Flame

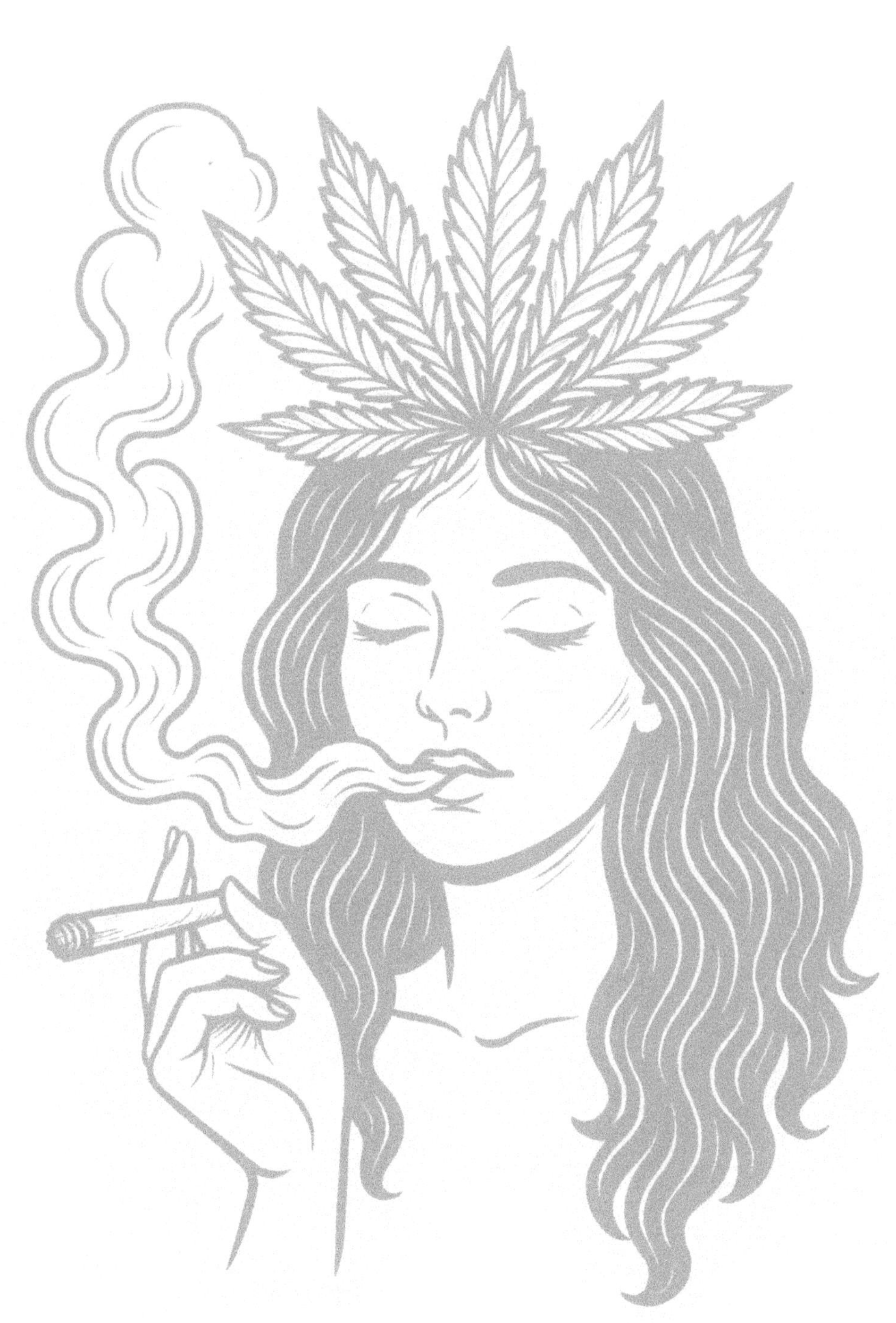

Float The Cloud

DRAW SOFT AND SLOW LIKE DRIFTING VAPOR.

EACH CURVE IS A BREATH—LET IT GO FREE.

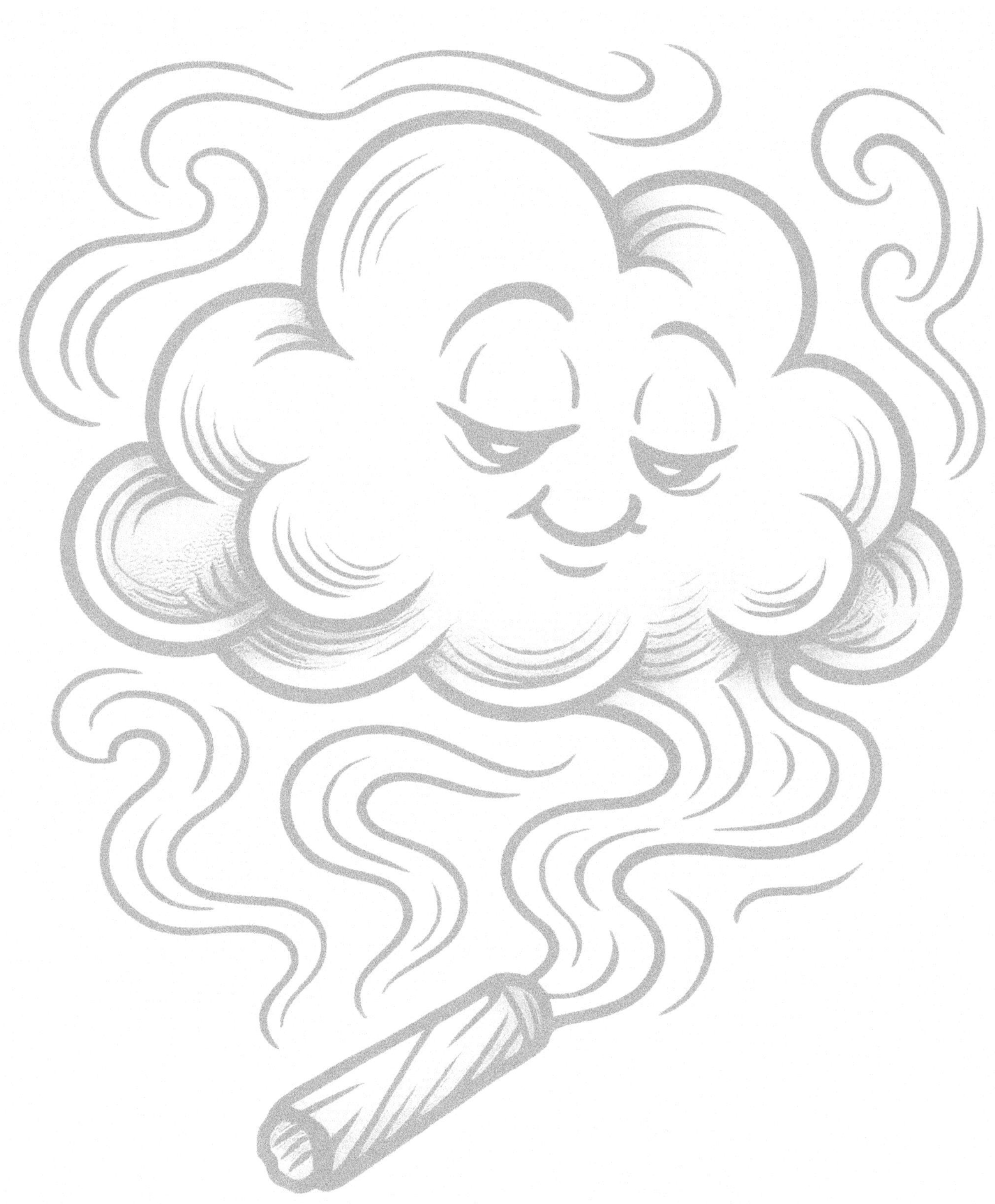

Light It Up

FOLLOW EVERY SPARK AND SWIRL.

TRACE LIKE SMOKE RISING WITH EVERY FLICK.

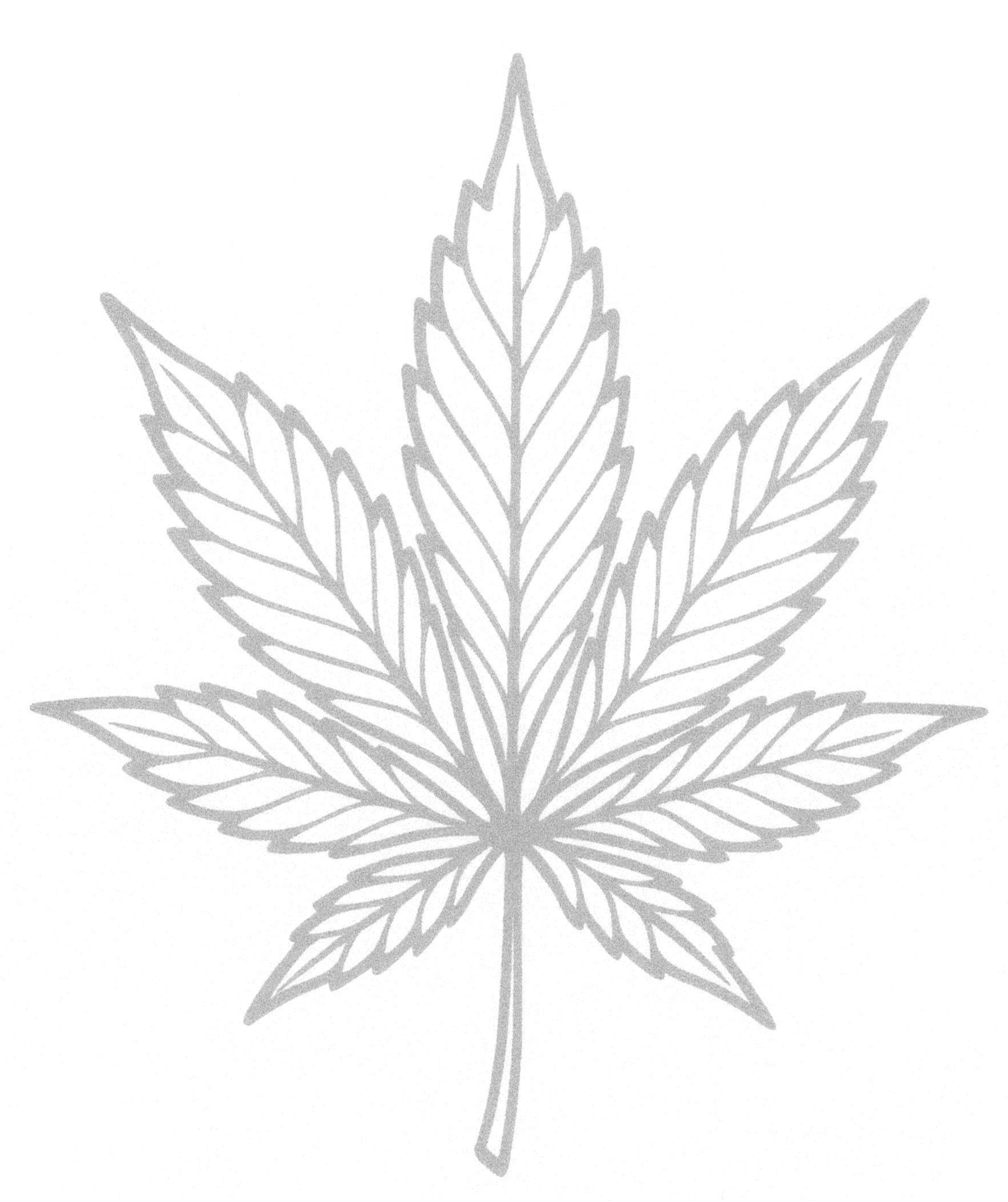

Stay Lifted

KEEP YOUR HAND LOOSE AND SPIRIT HIGHER.

TRACE THE VIBES—LET THEM RISE WITH EVERY LINE.

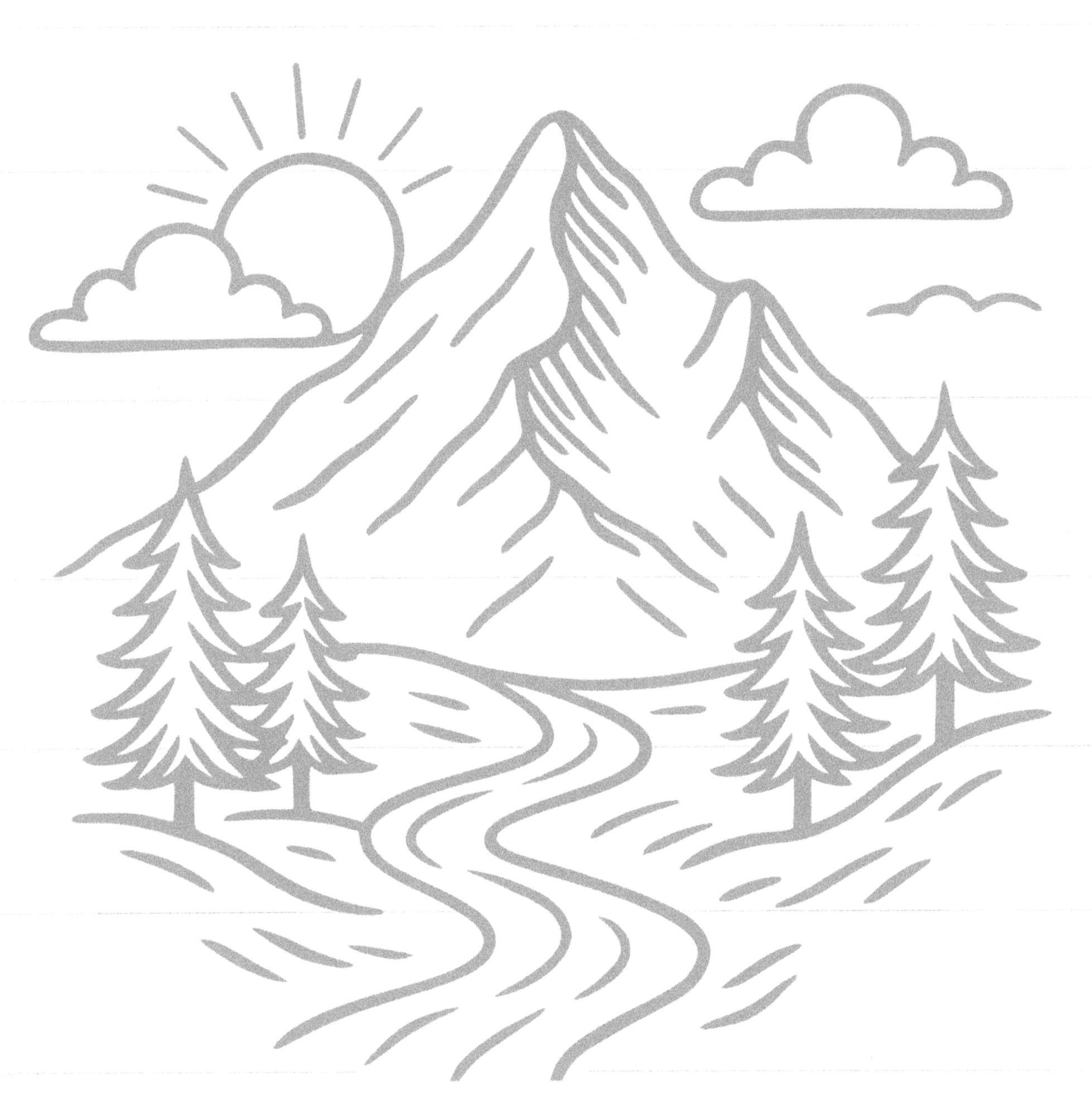

Cosmic Draw

TRACE THE UNIVERSE INSIDE YOUR MIND

LET EVERY LINE ORBIT WITH RELAXED INTENTION

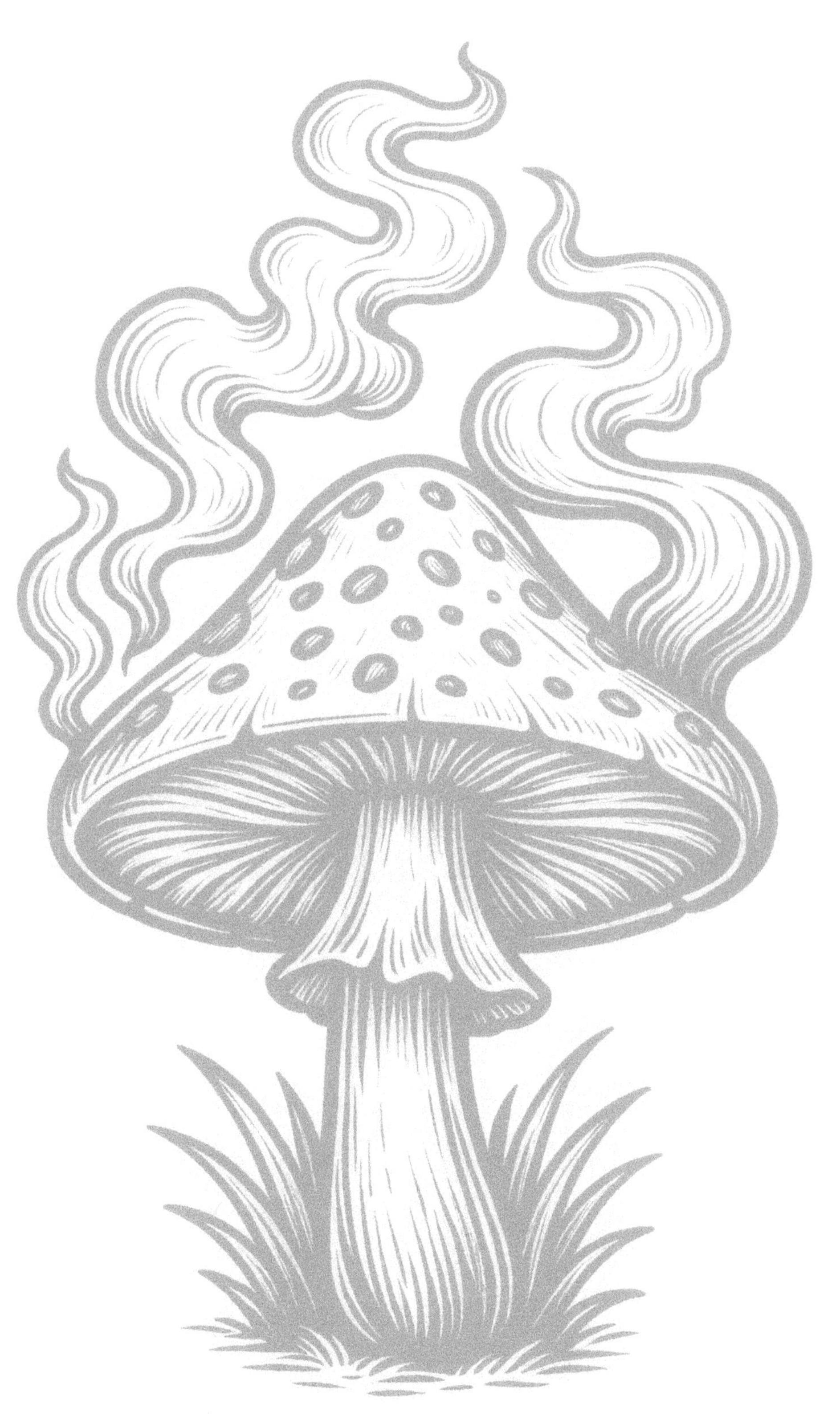

Grow The Bud

TRACE EACH PETAL AND LEAF LIKE IT'S BLOOMING.
TAKE YOUR TIME, FOLLOW NATURE'S RHYTHM

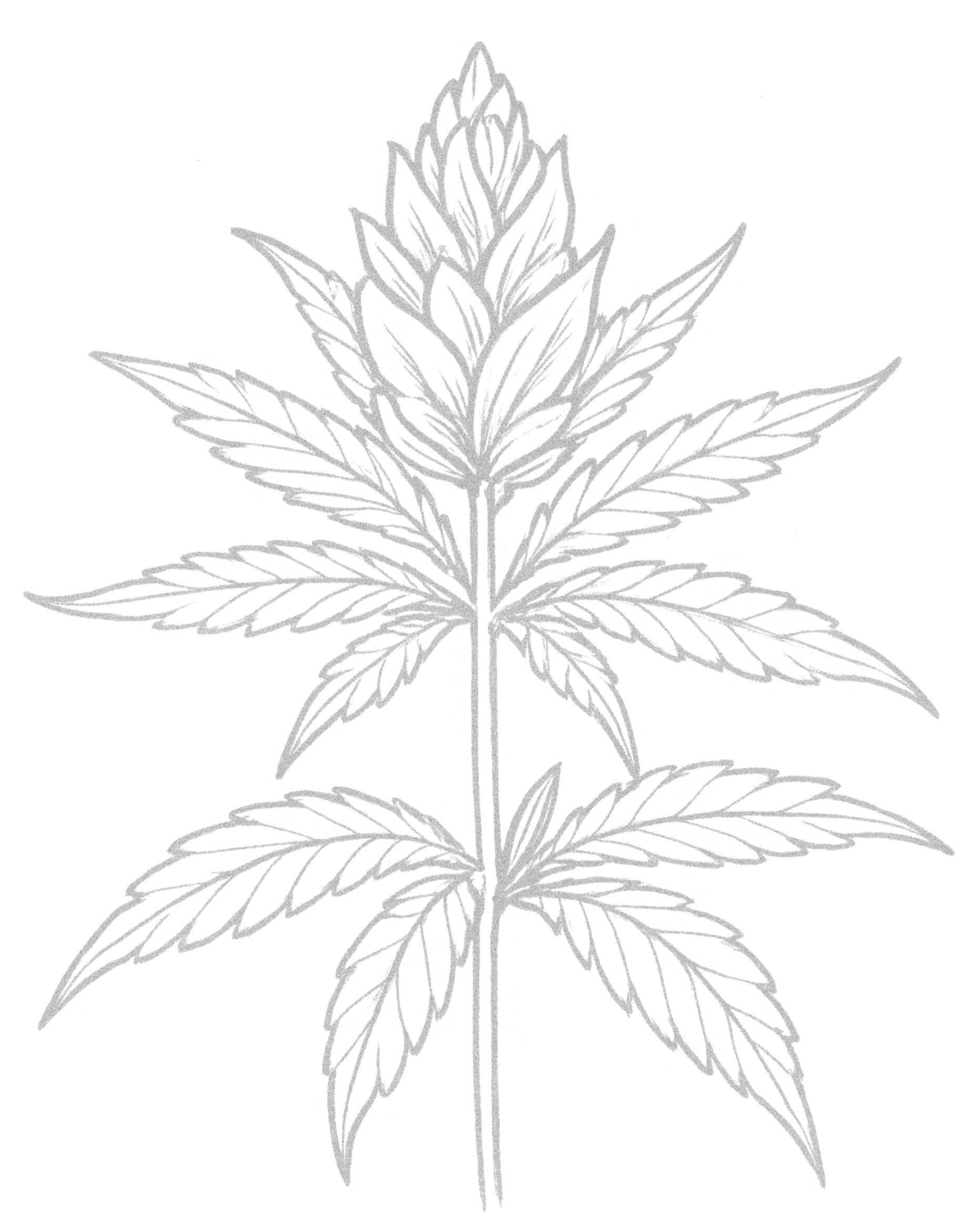

Chill the Skull

FOLLOW THE SHADOWS WITH SMOOTH LINES.

TRACE LIKE YOU'RE SCULPTING CALM FROM BONE.

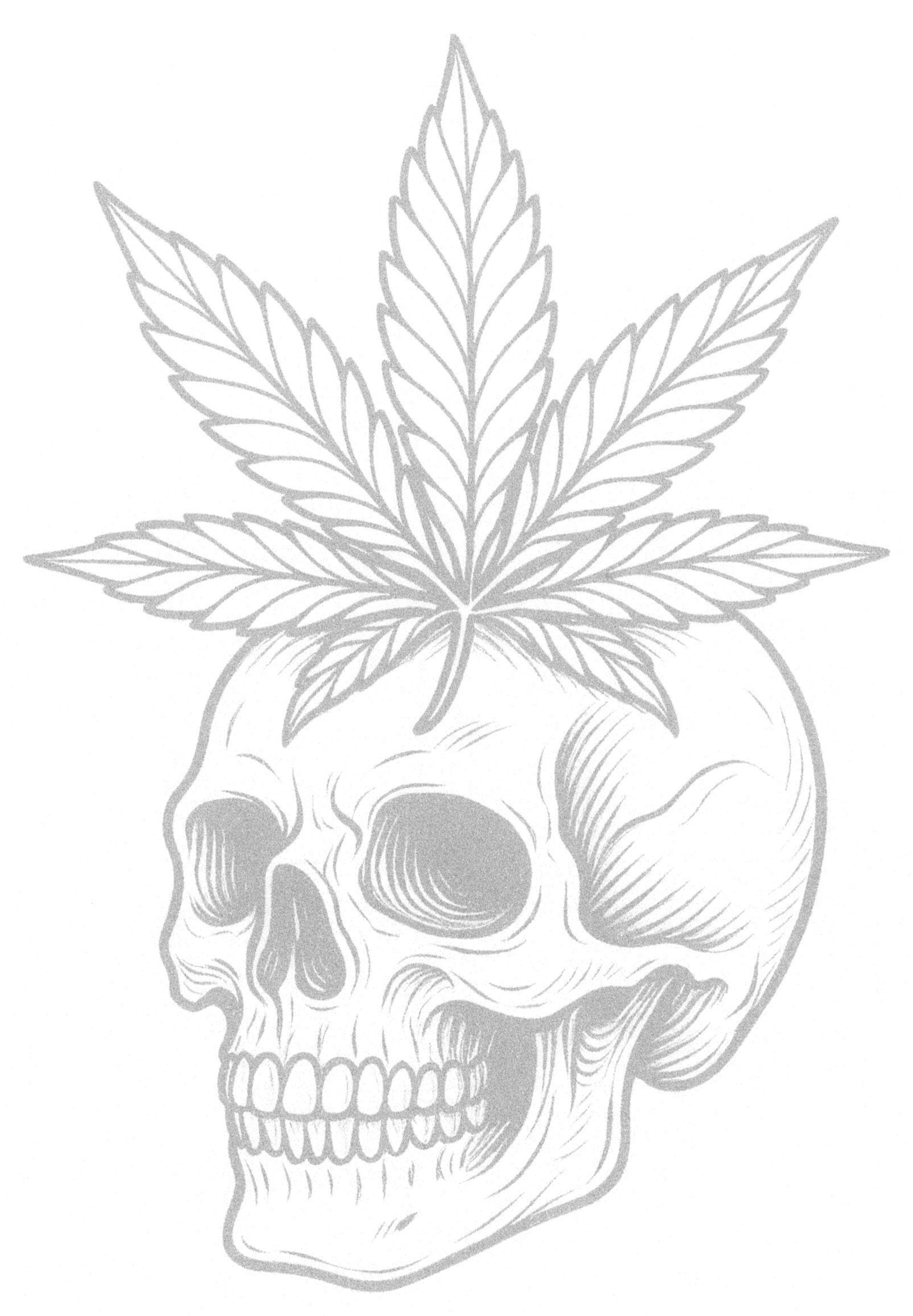

You Did IT, Legend!
You've reached the end of this trippy, inky
ride.

From letters to words, from vibes to full-on
chill phrases — your hand has grooved,
flowed, and traced through 60 pages of laid-
back creativity.

Calligraphy isn't about perfection.
It's about rhythm, mood, and letting the pen
dance like smoke in the breeze.

So roll with your style, spark up your ideas, and keep creating.

You've got the flow. Now let the world see it.

Stay lifted. Stay inspired. Keep writing.

Much love,
Your Chillest Ink Buddy